Copyright © 2020 by Freya K Ede

all despite the darkness

all despite the darkness

freya ede

to all those who take the time to support me and my work, thank you. i couldn't have done this without the overwhelming and intense support from all of you.

sarah, thank you for believing in me, i wouldn't have started this journey without you.

all despite the darkness

let me pour my pain
onto a page
and make
something so beautiful

contents

poetry is timeless
how i search for that hidden meaning
in everything they write
even if there isn't one to find

all despite the darkness

for when your heart is empty

all despite the darkness

i want to be more

than what my environment

makes me feel

like i am limited to do

who i used to be

tolerated that weapon

i used to think would save me

to protect myself

from the demons

descending from my own boiling blood

i rip the guilt from my existence

tearing apart skin

until i felt the release

of my own intentions

d

   r

     i

        p

down onto a past

clean from the splatters

of self-responsibility

my sense of self

is torn from the clean slate of my heart

through the moments of desperation i feel

as someone who tears their body apart

to feel what they once did

-alive

it's hard to find harmony

between you and the headspace

you find yourself confined in

slashing at the walls to open up

into a new beginning

free of the blame

which is always pointing at yourself

i want to disappear

to the times when the thoughts in my head

were the definition of innocence

not the essence of pain

caused by my own bare hands

the days i feel the most heartache

i don't have the energy to force the pain

i inflict on my own body

as revenge for the actions i see

the days where my heart sinks

to the bottom of my chest

allow me to break the barrier of torture

between me

and the mind that wants to destroy

the body it sits in

to feel something

once again

nothing breaks me quite like

the feeling of being subdued

left hollow

unable to ever be filled

again

its hard to sit here and lie

i'm always *just fine*

and its always *just good enough*

to make them believe it's really true

you want to know what angers me?

when they take my kindness

as a symbol of stupidity

a way of swerving around problems

being able to lie and manipulate

in a way i can't perfectly see

because my light is perfectly blurred

by the uniqueness

of my own over-giving soul

if only you had noticed the walls crumbling beside you
before they collapsed completely

if only they gave you the reassurance you needed
before you turned it all into self-doubt

certainty

is hard to cling onto

when your ropes are breaking

with every saw you take

at the threads holding you together

although i am nonchalant,

i show little emotion

my insides swell and my heart beats

just like any other human

i feel **intensely**

but showing it brings disappointment

no one sees me anyway

so whats the point in not hiding it

when the things i feel

remain to not change a single thing

i was betraying

my relationship with those i love

in the process of shaping myself

into someone who i never wanted to be

sometimes there's nothing more i want

than to carve the tender valleys

as i swim through the raw waters

of self-hatred and doubt

i feel my energy leak

into a pool of guilt

i gradually fill from the valleys

that start it all

-with my power filled hands

i can never stay comfortable

in my own skin for long

people crawl under

until i begin to lose myself

in everyone i love

recently

i feel myself spilling,

beginning to drip over a ledge

way beyond my concept of safety

and into a pool

of civilization

i had faded away

into the despair of my own

selflessness

as you engulfed yourself

in every bit of it you could find

skinning myself down,

im in a contest with who i am

and who they all want me to be

the body i set eyes on

wants to be set free

from everyone's expectations of what

someone like me should look like

i am disgust

in my eyes

and to every pair

staring at them

stretching my elastic skin

around to where

my eyes can't catch it

endlessly escaping my grip

and backstepping to where

it all was before

-where they all can see

i skin myself to bone

behind the scraped plates

clean

of suspicion form the cameras

flashing round my canvas

i hate to call mine

my heart sees hers in a new light

creating the glow of a thousand rays of light

beaming across my face

as her beauty

seeps into the most hollow

valleys caved into my body.

the earth separates us

like the sun and moon

always precisely out of reach

bouncing off of each other's surface

without truly touching

he dawns on me like the night

when all i can hope for is the day

-its not *him* i crave

how can i express the desire i feel

to entwine my freedom

with a woman

when they have built

walls with no windows

to watch her elegance shine through

i look at you

and see someone

willing to take care of everyone

but their own dying heart

no will *never* mean yes

the world surrounding me

bellows with such an aching silence

i can't take the simplicity of life

when you aren't ever really living it

in a place you can call home

with you no longer here

i will live my life through you, doing everything you would have done holding my hand

until you're there to greet me and i can hold it, for what feels like the very first time

life often feels like a train

i can never quite get on

one step forward, one step back

my face falls hopeless

watching the rest of the world being carried

ahead

right where they belong to be

leaving me behind

every single night

i stare at the same old crack

running down the centre of my ceiling

and it never changes

not after they say

it always gets better

it blurs into one

until i find myself

back at the same old crack in my ceiling

having moved nowhere

all despite the darkness

for when your heart is broken

all despite the darkness

you had showered me

in the safety

of the water you held.

it had washed away

once you no longer

drenched me in love

it was always so selfish

the day you decided to leave me again

it was always so selfish

for me to try and convince you to stay

you drank every truth

from my sweet soul

until you transformed me

into a girl

who had turned sour

even when i break my bones

to fit the conventions

that you make

you tell me

i'd never fit into a space

where i didn't belong

even the sun saw

the flame you scorched me with

when i was always the one who

turned the fire to ash

until the world finally noticed

the girl i once was

-she had burnt to the ground long before you saw

it will always break me

to know that the love you gave me

was only ever a fraction of what i truly deserved

yet i still picked up every little piece that i could find

gluing them together

until i had completely convinced my own dying heart

that it was being saved by one

that was just as whole as mine

but really, all it ever did

was pierce me with shards

which i never really

stopped trying to put back together

-it was never my job to fix you

my existence was ruled

by the words leaking

out of that wastepipe

i once kissed

to find the love

i was always looking for

i had left my

blood

sweat

tears

into a canister of appreciation

for you to carry round your neck

the tides had shaken

when the impact hit.

the breath i took away from my lungs

failed to fill yours

again, with new life

the shelter

that held me up-right

flew away

so, my barricades fell

crumbling

-without you anymore

there are often sunsets

where my heart

calls for yours

in return

i receive a glorious morning glow

projected by

mother nature herself

telling me your heart

no longer glows for my love

i want to scrub my mouth clean

my body clean

knowing your hands touched all of the places

they didn't deserve to go

you have been skinned

by the visions

of a perfect love

you ignored the reality

of what you were really receiving

the way the tides change

reflect the harmony between us

settling for a second

to finally feel comfortable

entwining through our bones

to find them

cracking apart from the refection

of who we both

want to be

the feeling of her skin is unmatched

by the soul which you handed to me

let me refresh time

so i can be there

in the depths with you

i feel as if the light

that once shone through my heart

to *her*

has once again been snatched by someone

who shines in the direction of my future

instead of my past

maybe we just are

soulmates

who were never meant to be

the life drained from my body

into the pool you dug for my love

and now,

i am numb

because of you

-a selfless love

what if i've been blinded

by the love i thought i needed for so long

to no longer see that

what i truly dream of in a person

is waiting for me

on the other side of the attachment

i can't quite let go of

i still look back

at who we once were

amongst the chaos

maybe i like the busy life,

maybe i just cant bear to give up

one more second

of my time

loving you

i distanced myself

for it is better to be sad without you

than happy with you

for a while

you have a heart that wants to be there for mine

in a way that i can't give

loving you would be dangerous

and that's why is better to be sad without you

than happy with you

for only a short while

because we both know

a while seems to leave people like us

too quickly

for love to begin to exist

your deep green eyes will always

take me through the flickers

of memories you've planted

in my head

ready to bloom

when my mind stumbles

upon the scent of flowers we grew

as one

-our short-lived cycle

to the one who got away,

i bled through

into someone else's love

just to feel the pressure

of the cloth

you used to press onto my wounds

when you re-opened my healed

scars

i used to believe

you held me unconditionally

in them arms

now i can see

you were holding my beating heart

to keep me from feeling

what spreading my wings really felt like

i let them tear drops

drench me

as you fell asleep alone

with me by your side

-it was only ever me

of course i wanted it to happen

i thought that was the language of love you spoke

until my body realised

the only way you kept me so close

was getting me to crawl inside your skin

don't take me for granted

i was a girl who took the weight

you willingly placed

upon her shoulders

you had taken her to the depths

to drown her in the secrets

you weren't yet ready to admit

i saved you

what did you see in me?

i was troubled from the start

i gave up every piece

one by one

until they filled your ego

high enough to breakaway

from a girl who saved your life

but crossed the finish line

with a destroyed one of her own

i only ever put pen to paper

when i envy the content of others

as i never thought you could leave me so easily

standing in the pouring rain

alone once again

left as a stranger to someone

who was a soulmate not yet meant to be

you see

i decided,

you never really took care

of the damage you caused

when you first broke the line of trust

between us

then you stitched it up

with your charm

and broke it for the second time

now im not coming back

i wrote about you.

it's not that easy to forget

when the cold air you let loose

is brushing across the pages of a book

full of hidden messages

about that wreck you left alone

you're now holding in the hands

which used to hold me

<u>i watched them leave</u>

why have you never learnt

that sour taste on your tongue

when i walk into the room

told you to find someone sweeter

instead,

you decided to cling onto the security

you found in my voice

until you stumbled across the courage

to murmur the words

telling me *its just too hard*

as you removed every bit of luck

from that essence you saw in my deep blue yes

by breaking the hand

you had resting on your shoulder.

when i looked into your eyes

i then saw a silhouette of a stranger destined

to pull apart my vision of a happy ending

in that moment i was overcome with the realisation

that i never should have expressed such gratitude

to someone who's able to

get up

and leave

why aren't you here?

you promised

i miss you

i miss the days we filled making memories together

i miss being able to find your comfort in all the things i did

i miss the life you breathed into my dying soul

i was belittled by hope and you restored my faith in love

i miss feeling like i was someone's first choice

i miss calling you mine when someone asks who you are,

i can only say your name now

i miss looking forward to a future with you,

and not one without

i miss seeing the love in your eyes when they stared into
mine

you made me start to love the pieces that had once fell

i miss feeling like i am not empty without you

who knew a song could bring everything back

but why am i surprised

i turned it on and turned it up

every time you made me feel broken

to remind myself of when my heart was intact

when i began to fall for you

right at the very start

you made it so easy for me

to see the real you

when you told me things

to my face

and betrayed them

as soon as you turned your back

if only you had fought to give me the love
i gave you

if only i hadn't given you my forgiveness
each and every time you lied to me

you're either in or out

in this twisted game

you showed no interest in playing

so why are you the one

dealing all the cards

destined to make me fall

back into your arms

again and again

loving you fulfilled me

as lungs need the air you breathe

i need the touch of your heart

so pure and gentle

to remind me of the love

i truly deserve

buttoned beneath the rubble

of how she once treated

honey,

maybe love wasn't built

for someone like you

who climbs the tallest walls

to reach the people who spend their time

knocking the bricks down

from the one you spent your entire life

building

no one else is warm enough to keep me from

the danger of not being free

in my own skin

out of fear from the stranger's eyes

that scour me for imperfections.

-i now feel safety in this skin

i feel so separated from my body

when i see her,

a body you have touched

to then inspect my own

and realise it will never

fill the beauty you

once saw in hers

it wasn't until the moon

i had always relied upon for hidden answers

fell behind the clouds that day

which you made me feel grey

i sat upon my windowsill

wishing it would shine full,

peer from behind the obscurity

and that's what would lead me to keep

fighting

maybe i did find disgust for you

that day

when you opened me in two

and expected me to heal

but when the night got cold

i dreamt of nothing more

but to have your hand traced

across my now broken body

even though it was you.

id like to say every time i paint you in my mind, the canvas is full of warmth, but something won't ever stop me from creating a canvas full of anger and pain, no matter how hard i look for what i really want to see.

the vision i had of you.

ever since the blindfold

they covered me with

was ripped away

you are the only one i seem to desire

in the solitude behind my closed eyes

they will come back in the emptiness

when it is no longer being filled

with your warmth

i caved into

the bottom of the earth

when the world broke my reality

of the life we were really going to lead

i find myself

once again

in the serenity of the night

all alone

without the one

trapped within me

are you still wishing
on a person who only bought you heartache?

they left and played the victim
to their own pre-meditated game

you meant a lot more to me

than i could ever show

you see,

if i pretend like i don't care

maybe with enough time

you'll start to fade

and ill finally be able to move on

my love for you flowered in the summer

projected through memories

each enlightened

by the sun that rose that day

as the sun started to sink below the depths of the

shifting seasons

i came only to see the memories

in the moments our love set

before the darkness that is,

now where our love stays

it seemed the dagger didn't slice you open, as it did me. it seemed that the flame didn't shine as bright, as it did for me. we were two people, too selfless to be who we wanted that when we collided, we couldn't fit each other as we were supposed to, after they broke us first. now i'm haunted by the ghost of you. and you continue without a shadow of me left. thank you for showing me that trust is something that can be broken. it's ironic really, the one thing you hold onto most can be misused by the people you never expect to rip it out your hands.

don't go breaking others too.

f.

the window hasn't changed,
and with the world moving forward
all it ever really does is bring me back
to you

the night you lied to me for the very first time,

thinking i wasn't human enough to understand

i could have torn apart my mind

deciding whether to leave or stay

knowing i was trusting the only piece of love

i was ever given

even if it'll drain me lifeless

in the end

i begun with your world in my hands

and left with a hollow space

where mine had been torn from my chest

and then taken by someone

who i don't think will quite ever give it back

you see,

the problem is that it was always just you holding every bit of
me

it will always break me
to know that the love you gave me
was only ever a fraction of what i truly deserved
yet i still picked up every little piece
that i could find
and glued them together
until i had completely convinced my own
dying heart
that it was being saved by one that was just
as whole as mine
but really, all it ever did
was pierce me with shards
which i never really
stopped trying to put back together

-it was never my job to fix you

it became a battle between pain and freedom

with you

i knew that i was numb

when i spent my time bleeding in a pool

of my own blood

rather than taking the pathway

that lead away from you

it became a battle between keeping and losing you

and i got wounded trying to keep the life

in a body so lifeless

it drained the feeling from mine

i lay on my back, staring at the same old sky
painted in a dirty shade of white
with a crack finding its way right through the middle
i emerge myself in disbelief as i pretend its *that night*
when you held me under the stars,
and the emptiness almost felt whole
my tears had a palm to fall into.
except the sky is no longer reflects the atmosphere of our
love
to no surprise, the sky remains plain
left without a mark, except a crack
breaking right through the middle.

now i stand still within a timeline, no longer between a life
with you and me
where your finger could ever so carefully catch the fall of a
tear shed, falling down my cheek.
now i'm faced with the reality of laying on my back under a
poorly painted ceiling
just as you left us
slowly crumbling under a past i visit often
under a sky that will never quite resemble the memories of
you and me.

it's just like you to excuse

all the little things you did

telling me it's okay, *you love me*

until i crawl right into your skin,

until you forget to want to hold me

in the way you used too

because deep down you know

that you will always know you broke me

and i broke you too

i spent my time

collecting every single thing we needed

to build a home

through times old ways, it's beginning to crumble

and i can't find the strength to save it

not this time

a pit

sits so deep within me

i loved you for the very last time

with a love you never began to feel

it's as if you held my heart in your hands and crushed it in front of my eyes. but the feeling of your touch was always enough to convince me to bargain my dying heart for what i had always needed. someone to hold me.

my lonely heart was never made to meet someone as invasive as you and now you are just a stranger who knows me in the way a lover should our love wasn't perfect,

as it always goes

it only reaches halfway across yours

and fully around mine

i begged you to love me

the love i craved

was always a step away

from the love you could afford to give

i begin to wonder how much of my love

ever belonged to you.

where did you find the space to misplace it,

when i spent every effort piecing it together

to fit you

and you only.

today i heard *our* song for the first time since, and for the first-time music didn't feel like an escape

i can't comprehend how you must feel, to know you broke
the heart of a girl who began to think the love you gave her
was real. when it was all just <u>abuse</u>.

i cannot wrap my head around

how badly you needed me

but how little you ever tried

to make me stay

you pushed the guilt down my throat until i felt bad enough
to never go

<u>the morning after</u>

i woke up not knowing why

my face was worn and swollen

then my mind stopped to grieve the fact

i no longer have you here with me

all despite the darkness

...and now we are strangers again

all despite the darkness

for when your heart is full

all despite the darkness

i went home and told her

the aches of my past have been freed

with my new angel

letting me spread my wings

as i open hers.

why do you let another roam your sky?

her words found me from a place

that genuinely touches

my heart

i hear your heart speaking to mine

with a language only we know

the truth will always be that i remain soulless without you. we all have parts that make a whole. it just happened to be that you showed me what owning my own heart felt like, by handing me the other half.

i have indulged myself

into a soul

that understands

the very complexity

of mine

it's almost as if the silent cries

that i project into the moon

are soaked up by you

when your eyes catch the beam

of its reflection,

of my wish

if only you knew the way i have fallen for you

my mind conjured together the

parts of love i feel with you

to discover my ridged edges turned smooth

as you cradle me in the love

i always deserved

i look up at the moon

and feel less alone

as if your eyes

are also searching for my shadow

in her reflection

i want to hold your soul
in the palm of my hands
to see all the imperfections
perfectly imperfect
to me

your elegance

freed its way into my mind

driving it to a place

where i can view

a place so generous and warm

projecting a sunrise

as ethereal as the words

you speak to me

i like to think

we were aligned somewhere in the universe

made to meet under a star

and just as it is destined to burn out,

so were we

as its light could no longer stand

to be lit by our broken hearts

forever is never quite long enough

to sit there

and gather every feeling you give me

and make sense

of just how much i love you

you asked me to tell you

that i loved them

without spilling the three words

as i always do

i told you

they are everything that makes me complete

her eyes

tell me all the answers

my whole life

was consumed in confusion

until her angel wings

shielded me from the pain that

needed to be healed

from within

it didn't take me long to realise

love isn't made of red roses.

its who is gentle enough to pick up

all the petals

as they fall

so they have the strength bloom again

generosity flows so freely in you

like the way rain

has to pour

to water what is trying to grow

you watered me

and so patiently stayed

to watch me bloom

if heaven is you

then being sent to hell

knowing i'm yours

and you are mine

will be an eternity

i am willing to live through

our lives simply aren't long enough to spend forever

with you

and if i could live one life for me

and one for you

i would feel a little less weight on my shoulders

knowing i have given you more time

to explore the world that was created for you

and loving you is always so painfully beautiful.

and i was told

the touch of his lips

would eventually bring me to heaven

but for the first time in my life

i hadn't minded

the possibility

of touching hers

might bring me to hell

serenity

was flowing through her

until she held me

so gently

sparking me to embrace every flaw

she had ever seen

and allowed it to

freely flow through me

-through us

as i slip into those hazel eyes

the autumn seasons

changes to the warm glow of summer

engulfing my glowing heart

falling into a promising future

you reflect the world

through those blue eyes

as i see every detail

in the gaze i know will never grow old

it forever flows

freely in my heart

you give me the gift of safety
in your silence

i thought about losing you

and every bone in my body

crumbled to the floor

as my home got destroyed

before it just entered my grasp,

dust starts slipping through my fingers

delicately

my palms cradling

what you leave behind

maybe there's not much place for us with God in heaven

but i certainly know that in a world where i shouldn't believe it's true

i'm certain that he made you

to belong perfectly in hell with me

i feel so invisibly empty

imagining what it feels like

to be cradled in your arms

when i realise

you are only ever able to

put every piece of me together

without the reality

of being half a world away

-long distance

you are my person

your eyes hit my face

like the sunlight you find

falling onto your face

in early spring

as the flowers in me emerged,

a subtle shade of pink

one that you planted there

to take care of

until they bloomed

in early summer

and in that moment

there was

me and you

for the rest of eternity

i convinced myself

i was content with loneliness

until i found a soul

made for mine

simply

hidden under them dimples

i now call home

the thing i will always want you to know,
to engrave in your mind
somewhere
no matter how many imperfections fall through
into the love that we hold
keep your grip tight
because every bit of me will continue to love you
for every imperfection you carry
with you

i see perfection in you.

just like the moon saw

as he birthed me

and patiently watched me grow

into a girl

just wanting another to love her

in the same way

she sees nothing short of beauty

in every single place on earth

maybe we are a sin,
maybe our souls were meant to burn together

you're familiar

like my soul years ago

we were looking for you

so we could embrace the scars

we have both been embellished in

so they can be covered in a safety

we both dreamed of long ago

you simply inspire me

to become the most me

and to allow you

to become the most you

that you will ever be

water me

and watch me bloom

as i pick my blossom

and tuck it behind your ear

so you can feel beauty too

-mutual

tomorrow the sun

will touch the horizon

and the sky will blush

with a shade i can only dream of painting across your face

as i stare into your eyes

and find myself falling

all over again

the sun

on bare skin

where your hands have been

feels almost as good

but not the same

because you're not there

-long distance

the moon waited his whole life

to watch us meet

to begin our eternity

and his lifelong romance

you have captured me

and with my old

broken voice

all i can ask

is that you never let me go

my mind races a million seconds at a time
thinking of a life without you
and the ending i always find myself at,
the future is forever changing, but the one thing that stays is
always you.

the taste of his lips

will always be bitter

when hers

taste like fresh honey

i know that in this lifetime

we have made a myriad of mistakes

and aren't without a little less than perfection

the truth is, i will be there for you

either way

i know that if you are the only perfect thing

i can begin to hold onto for life

then all of them mistakes, leading me to you

become a little more significant each and

every time

but

her lips

are the sweetest things

i have ever tasted

today they asked me to define beauty, and i swear that it is *you* in the purest form

i love you

in an infinite way

as if every version of me

and every version of you

have found each other

in every other life

when we least expected love

at a time it was most needed

i wish i could

tell you i love you.

i hope

you look into my eyes

as i walk away

and see every single reason

my heart longs to stay

if the sky was falling

and in our conscience

both knowing

it will have all ended

before it even started

i simply be on top of the world

to have felt the touch of your love

in the probability

of this lifetime

to be held in your arms

as it all crumbles below us

i could not feel more blessed

to end on the very bottom

of our own world

even though

i still feel at the very top

loving you is the most significant thing i will ever do
because you are the only one
who sees me

serendipity is the awe i feel as i see your face

i am always so grateful to know,

as without this energy

drawing me towards you

from the pure angelic

life that you breathe into me

serendipity could not exist

as you,

are that in itself

you are my green

everything feels so serene with your presence

the connection i feel with nature

falls over me

like the delicacy in rain

as it hydrates the earth

bringing it to life again

there is never a break in the trust

they hold as two

and before you every emotion i felt was a projection of what i wanted it to be, not what it actually was. now being loved is a reality.

i don't usually call myself lucky with things

they always find themselves just

within my reach

when i began to feel you closer than most

i turned my head behind,

not to see you metres away

i turned my head to feel your hand

placed against my skin

for once you weren't within my reach

i was in yours

and it is pure luck

to be so entirely consumed by a girl

i hadn't spent a lifetime chasing

even the sensation of a million stars colliding couldn't quite
capture how it feels to be in this moment with you

my heart beats to be able to spend a lifetime loving you

i stare too much

not because of how beautifully perfect you are,

which don't get me wrong, is true

but because i am in awe

of everything you do.

the truth is,

i don't think i've ever met someone so perfect for me

in every way that's more than just physical

your beauty comes from within

and it has completely taken over

what i thought love once was

all despite the darkness

for when your heart is healing

all despite the darkness

<u>we are beauty</u>

why should the hair on my body

be a deciding factor

with that small-mindedness of yours

for whether i am deemed

a woman

worth the attention of a man

did no one ever tell you

the lines mapped out

across every curve you wear

with such beauty

sends out the brightest smile to others

who wear them with shame

-confidence waters every dying flower

i'll be there eventually

to cradle you

back into the peace

of being with my soul again

i'm on my journey

i'm coming home

i don't need

your validation

to mould me into a girl

only defined by your opinions

i am my own woman

i began to think that you were

the light rain after the storm

soaking me under the peace

it brings

i can now see

that you were the beginning

that rumbled ahead of us

you have fallen into a sky of downpour,

i have risen as a rainbow

my energy is admirable

by those who own a sour

drenched ego

the sun's rays

bow before my radiant glowing skin

for mother nature

is most generous to those

who provide her with the energy of

everlasting love

the incomparable desire

to be my own consumes me

as i stride through my present

and make my own future

be patient with my heart
it is still healing

this story planned ahead of me

writes itself with every new day

i am told to live

why allow yourself to be pushed

into living a life by a writer

who knows nothing of

the plot you dream

to experience

-let go of those who define you

we are all just angels on our way

back home

to something we each are drawn too

some of us just spread our wings early

after all,

who else would reach for our hand

and welcome us into our new home

sometimes the thing you want most in this world is that which is the furthest reach from where you find yourself now. in the end, that's what keeps us here, fighting, knowing at the end of this path, no matter which you choose, you will be one step closer to that which you felt ever so far away from. so, don't be scared of what tomorrow brings, it may be a long way down yet but its closer to home than yesterday.

redefine

the life you now embrace

after surrendering to the one

you lost a hold of

-be free

take the flame

that blisters you now

and use it to guide your way

to a beginning with a self-projected light

instead of using it as a way

to destroy your own skin

today may not be what you want

but it will always be time

to find the happiness

you need in

tomorrow

sometimes you need to realise

you can still find the beauty

stemmed in the things

that end up to the temporary

in the end

it makes you cherish it

just that little bit more

i knew the wound that had been seeping

my own worth

had closed up when

i laid in my own emptiness

touching my heart

and i felt it beat, finding a home

without you guiding it to where it was hiding,

underneath who i truly deserve to be

-i am my own home

we may all be sinking

below the water line

in our own boats

but we are all in the eye

of the

exact   same   storm

your heart stands alone

but together,

they all beat as one

tonight i was consumed

by this newfound freedom

you handed to me

i forgot to urge myself into the old routine

i felt so confined to follow

under your rules

as time continues to move forward

in a direction against me

i can say

it gets better the further you travel

for each day they are on your mind

another will pass without

before your soul is aware

the thought of them will drift by

as a distant past time

you no longer reach to grasp

but instead

you cherish

before it washes away

once more

-our almost love

from me to you

find your worth

because i promise you

its more than how they make you feel

its more than how they treat you

its more than how you see yourself

your worth

is everything

your worth

deserves

the love you give others

you are worth more
than how they use you

the fresh air brushes over

this simple life of mine

in nature's eyes as i stand with my feet

pressed against her heart

worrying about the sunrise

she plans for tomorrow

i didn't sit here today

to complain that tomorrow

is about to indulge its

disappointment onto me

i sat here today wanting to know

the promises tomorrow can bring

as i let myself go

submerging into the depths

of another ocean

full of curiosity

no one is ever truly alone

we are kept together by the moons appearance

each night

look at him and know

you arent the only pair of eyes

lost amongst this world full of souls

longing to be found

you see if you believe there is no hope in tomorrow

you find yourself believing

yesterday's worry

every single time you convinced yourself

that you could not make it

you opened your eyes to a fresh day

with new hope and new intentions

set out there

in front of you

you remain

here

with yourself

in one piece

if only you handed yourself the love

you spend so much of giving to others

if only you took a second

to see the beauty you behold

i am free

to collect the pieces

and fill this new beginning of mine

until the brim overflows

with the hopes i dreamt of

in a past life

with you

you closed the cycle

we had begun to loop together

but did you realise

it was when you let me go

my new beginning only

just began

she is the kind of girl

who sees beauty

in everyone

there is love in patience

there is patience in forgiveness

there is good

even in the most evil of things

it's not finding it that's hard

its accepting that our souls

are equally as ready

to grow as another

you are the light

after the darkness

soak yourself in golden warmth

and

let them taste them honey sweet lips

you are so beautifully unaware

of how you make everything bloom

and everyone flourish

one thing i have always admired about the sun is her willingness to reappear, with us relying on her light. she can be hidden away and shielded by all the things that make her days unseeable. but you see, she is the perfect metaphor for growth. she soon begins to outgrow the earths horizon until she appears brighter than ever, to cover us in the goodness she provides. mother nature sees the pain in people. look up at the sky and see a message to spread love. growth isn't linear, neither is the pattern of the earth.

i knew my anger was gone

when i could hear our song

and the lyrics made me feel whole

instead of a lacking

of someone i always hoped id find

in a song i only ever sang

before our love faded

let it go,

flowers have to fall

to flourish

at the end of it all

i don't regret a thing

you taught me to see the difference

between the idea and the reality

of loving someone who loved you back

and now i won't spend another second

of my time

pursuing the expectations in someone

who i never deserved

in the first place

what was always clear to them, seemed blurred to her

she spent her whole life wondering why she was different

if only she had realised

what she sees clearly

is what they see out of focus

she was different

and if only she had understood

that everyone wished they could have seen as clearly as her

let the dust settle

allow yourself to see clearly again

never let them cloud your vision

of whom you know you need to be

-you dictate your own future

hold your own hand

to find yourself dancing again

under a sun

that was always there, shining down on you

so you can glow

once again

dry your tears, like you did before

with every end there is a new song

waiting to be sung

in a voice so pure

as life brings you to a new beginning

to dance through again

and your heart was made to love those who give you light

not the ones who shade it from being who it truly wants to be

grief is endless

what is not, is the life you live

the sky will shine once again

with a palette they have created

as they water you with heart filled rain

watching you getting ready to bloom

in a life

without them anymore

a pinpoint

is where you stand

amongst thousands of days

you have to heal

be a shoulder you can cry on

through days where you feel so unsure of yourself

even when the world falls through your hands

you will always know

pain comes and goes

through the wind and the rain

the scars always fade away

and the smile on your face

smiles along with the sun

which never quite left your side

-you'll have yourself always

sometimes a new chapter isn't the end of one

you didn't want to stop writing

it's the beginning of the something

which will be the more amazing thing

you'll ever be a part of

flowers grow to fall

heartaches build up to break

but a flower always opens again

just as a heart continues to beat

realising they *had* control over you is the first step in understanding that you are able to let go. letting go always seems so unimaginably hard but when you see the potential of meeting the hand of another, waiting to give you the love you have always deserved, its simply falling away from someone who was stupid enough to give you a reason to no longer hold on and falling into the arms of someone who will never give you a reason to leave.

with every depth you are submerged within

you are given the chance to swim back to the surface

and breathe again,

take it

-don't let life drown you

try once more,

this time might be the one

a broken heart is one worth healing, its life's way of showing you the strength you have don't for a second, doubt the sound of that heart

carrying you through life

it knows what it wants

and it's your job

to guide it there

there is no space to stop

when the world is waiting for you

to

go

and

live

in

it

pour your love

into someone

who truly deserves a new

replenished kind of love

in you is a girl willing to fight

again and again

until she finds what she's truly meant for

take the pain as a sign to move on

to something so much more gentle

to your soul

as we both know

the pain will leave

and the healing will appear again

when you are fed up with seeing nothing

but the dark side of the world,

light will always catch up with you

even on the days you dread

you will wake up to a sun that will never fail to rise

here you are,
the person you have become despite it all

i'm beginning to understand,

it's now time for me to leave

as the dust begins to settle

revealing a fresh pattern, a new pathway to follow

for us to go our separate ways

releasing the hurt

weighing heavily on our hearts

giving us both the road ahead to heal

my body will never be defined by the one

you say it was born into

i was always me

and i will always grow up to be someone

worth expressing themselves

in the body

they want

there will always be a calm after the storm.

why are you hiding your true colours

when your palette is the most beautiful

that i have ever seen

you will not write my future for me.

i will not let your actions bleed through

into this life i have a chance to live

i will not let the way you treated me stop

the way i want to grow

you are no longer here

to restrain me

i am finally free

to live again

thank you for finding my heart once again, spread across these pages. you have the strength in you to heal just as i did. you will get there, in time. just know you are not alone on this journey, it might look undefeatable now, but once you've pushed yourself to that place you need to be, life will become beautiful again. you will do it all despite the darkness.

thank you with my whole heart

-a letter from someone who cares, freya.

this is only the beginning

Printed in Great Britain
by Amazon